Robin's Raspberries

Once upon a time there was a teddy
bear called Robin who loved to see
dolphins in the ocean and to play,
especially on the beach.

Robin also loved growing raspberries.

One day Robin wanted to go to the local market for a cake. There were a lot of different people selling very yummy fruits and vegetables.

Robin was fascinated by all of the different colours- the strawberries and raspberries were red, cucumbers were green, carrots were orange and aubergines were purple. Selling fruits and vegetables looked like fun.

Robin's parents noticed Robin's interest and asked if Robin wanted to learn more about running a business. Robin eagerly nodded, excited to learn more.

So, Robin's parents started teaching the basics of running a business: how to do maths, how to set goals, and how to market products to be profitable.

Robin was a quick learner and soon started implementing everything learned, including making a plan for the raspberry stand and setting a goal to sell 20 punnets of raspberries in one day. This would give Robin enough profit for a trip to the ocean.

Robin's Raspberries

Robin was ready to sell the raspberries grown in the garden. Robin's parents helped create a sign to advertise the raspberry stand and Robin even designed a logo for the business.

On the day of the raspberry stand
opening Robin was so excited! The
stand was set up, the sign was placed,
and Robin waited for customers to
come. Soon, other teddy bears started
to come and Robin greeted them with a
big smile. Robin's parents were there to
supervise.

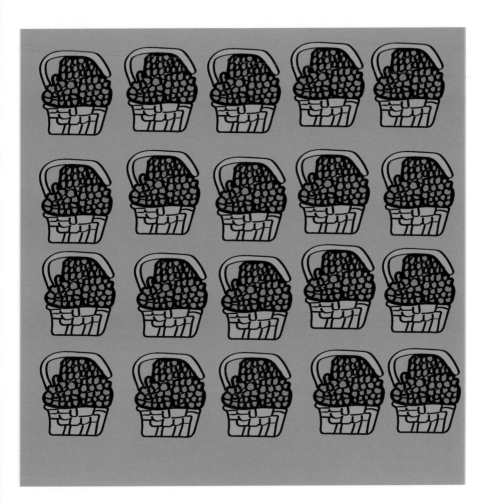

Robin's raspberry stand was a big success! Teddy bears loved it and started telling their friends about Robin's stand. Before too long Robin had sold all 20 punnets of raspberries and even had some repeat customers.

Robin was very happy with the result of hard work and determination and couldn't wait to grow other lovely fruits and vegetables to sell.

From that day on Robin continued to run the fruit and vegetable stand and even started to expand the business by selling chickpeas, lentils and beans.
Robin had become a young entrepeneur and was well on the way to becoming a successful business person.

Robin used the profit to sail away on holiday. Robin was excited to see dolphins swimming near them.

Robin had lots of fun playing on the beach.

Printed in Great Britain
by Amazon

25703818R00016